Affiliate Marketing

A Comprehensive And Sequential Guide For Novices All The Necessary Resources For Harnessing The Profitability Of Affiliate Marketing

(Accelerate Earnings By Engaging In Online Promotion Of Amazon Affiliate Program Offers)

Murray Clarkson

TABLE OF CONTENT

Introduction To Affiliate Marketing 1

Steps To Attain Super Affiliate Status 13

Where Is Your Customer 32

What Are The Qualities Of An Effective Affiliate Program? 51

Selecting Suitable Affiliate Programs: A Guide To Making An Informed Choice 84

How To Initiate The Establishment Of An Affiliate Marketing Enterprise 97

Advantages Of Affiliate Marketing 110

Comprehending The Payment Mechanism Utilized By Clickbank 131

Strategies For Prudently Evaluating Affiliate Products And Making Informed Decisions 140

Introduction To Affiliate Marketing

Becoming involved in the field of affiliate marketing has become highly accessible due to the widespread availability of the Internet. It is notably more convenient in present times compared to an era wherein individuals had to rely on telecommunication devices and additional forms of media to acquire timely updates on the progress of their programs. Considering the availability of the technology and if your partner works remotely, a typical day in your life would resemble the following.

Upon awakening, I proceed to have breakfast and subsequently power on my computer to peruse the latest online updates. For marketers, there may be a need to update new articles and monitor statistical data. It is necessary to make alterations to the design of the website. Marketers are aware that a meticulously crafted website has the potential to enhance visitor registration. In addition, it can contribute to improving your affiliate conversion rate. Once you have completed the necessary steps, it is imperative to proceed with the submission of your affiliate program to a reputable directory that provides comprehensive listings of affiliate programs. This directory serves as a means to entice individuals to partake in your affiliate program. A highly effective approach to enhance the visibility of your affiliate program!

Presently is the opportune moment to diligently and precisely monitor your affiliate sales. We offer the convenience of tracking your orders through both telephone and email correspondence. Ensure that there is a steady influx of potential customers observing your product. Please record your contact information, as it may prove to be a valuable asset in the future.

There exists a multitude of resources available for your perusal. Advertisements, banners, interactive display advertisements, and promotional incentives that marketers recognize as effective methods to augment sales. It is equally beneficial to ensure its visibility and accessibility. It is important for affiliate marketers to bear in mind that visitors may have inquiries that require attention. This task must be expedited. An unresponsive email has the potential to greatly dissuade customers.

Additional focus should be dedicated to addressing the inquiry, as it serves as a demonstration of the effectiveness and efficiency of the partnership. Being disregarded is undesirable, and it is worth noting that the customer does not invariably possess unlimited patience. An expeditious reply that exudes a sense of professionalism and approachability. Upon meeting all the necessary criteria, the marketer gains access to the chat room where they engage in communication with fellow partners participating in the same program. They have the opportunity to engage in discussions regarding the enhancement of their product's promotion. There exist opportunities for acquiring knowledge and this is a continual endeavor. The act of exchanging tips and advice serves as a significant means of expressing support. Others may desire to participate and engage in a discussion. There is no detriment in capitalizing on the opportunity that presents itself. The recent update of the newsletter and e-magazine necessitates affiliate marketers to assess the latest offerings available in the market. This information will be documented in the marketer's publications and disseminated to both existing and prospective customers. In addition, these publications serve as a vital resource for staying informed about recently introduced products. Marketers have orchestrated sales and advertising endeavors that have piqued the interest of customers, prompting them to seek further information. It is imperative that you also meet the sales deadlines explicitly stated in the publication.

It is incumbent upon marketers to express gratitude to those individuals who have played a pivotal role in generating sales and facilitating promotional initiatives. There is no greater joy than commemorating an individual, their online platform, and the intricate process that paved the way for its realization. Undoubtedly, this information will be duly referenced in the forthcoming newsletter. Included in the pertinent written material.

Marketers still have the opportunity to craft proposals for individuals seeking a reliable source for their advertising products. In addition, we possess sufficient time to express our perspectives regarding the strategies to thrive as an accomplished affiliate marketer on renowned online platforms. Simultaneously, two objectives were successfully accomplished. Marketers have the ability to market and advertise both the products and programs in which they are involved. Who knows? Some may participate. Time flows. I regrettably did not have the opportunity to partake in lunch, however, I am content with the progress made in my work. bedtime....

Understandably, it may not be feasible to complete everything within a single day. Nonetheless, it provides affiliate marketers with insight on how they allocate resources on specific marketing days. Could you please clarify if it is merely a fortunate coincidence or if there are specific reasons behind this occurrence on the street?

Flourish and persist as an affiliate marketer

Nowadays, every affiliate marketer perpetually seeks a lucrative market that presents the utmost financial gains. Occasionally, I ponder over what seems to be an enchanting amalgamation that renders them effortlessly attainable. Indeed, the matter at hand is of a more intricate nature than initially perceived. They are great marketing practices proven through years of hard work and dedication. There exist strategies that have proven effective in the realm of Internet marketing historically and continue to remain relevant in the domain of affiliate marketing at present. The following recommendations encompass three highly effective marketing strategies that possess the potential to augment your sales and ensure your endurance within the realm of online affiliate marketing.

The three tips

Utilizing distinct web pages dedicated to promoting and advertising each individual product within your marketing initiative.

Avoid amalgamating all aspects for the purpose of economizing on web hosting. It is advantageous to possess a dedicated website centered around each individual product. It is advisable to incorporate product reviews on your website in order to provide visitors with an initial understanding of the product's capabilities and the benefits it offers to potential buyers. Additionally, it is important to incorporate testimonials from individuals who have successfully utilized the product. Please ensure that you consent to the utilization of your name and image on the website associated with the particular product you are vending.

One may also compose articles that showcase the utilization of the products and incorporate them as supplementary pages within the website. Enhance the visual appeal of your page while incorporating a request for the exchange of information. Every headline should serve to entice readers to delve further into the content or establish contact with your organization. Please take note of your unique characteristics. This aids readers in gaining comprehension and cultivating a desire for further exploration of the page's content.

Extend complementary reports to your target audience.

If feasible, place it at the topmost section of the page to ensure prominent visibility. Develop an automated responder system which promptly sends emails to individuals who voluntarily submit their personal details through the opt-in box. Studies indicate that the process of finalizing sales commonly occurs subsequent to the seventh interaction with a prospective customer.

There are only two possibilities that can occur on a web page. Sales that have been finalized or prospects who depart from the Page and do not revisit. By subsequently sending valuable information directly to their email inbox, it will aid in reinforcing their memory of the product they previously expressed interest in, thus ensuring that they are aware of the conclusion of the sale. Ensure that your content exhibits a clear emphasis on a distinct rationale for making a purchase. Please refrain from presenting it in a manner reminiscent of a promotional pitch.

Direct your attention to important aspects, such as the ways in which your product facilitates convenience and enhances enjoyment in various aspects of life. Include a captivating subject line in your email. Minimize the usage of the term "free" to the greatest extent feasible. Due to the utilization of outdated spam filters which effectively eliminate such content prior to its consumption by any individual. Persuade your subscribers who have access to your complimentary report that they are overlooking significant benefits if they do not utilize your products and services.

Acquire the type of targeted traffic aligned with your product.

If the products you offer fail to capture the interest of your website visitors, it is likely that they belong to the category of non-returning visitors. Produce written content for publication in periodicals and digital publications. By following this approach, you can discover posts that are specifically tailored to your target audience, and the content you share may also capture your interest.

Produce a minimum of two articles per week, each comprising 300 to 600 words in length. Through consistent composition and upkeep of these articles, you can effectively draw in hundreds of target readers to your website on a daily basis. Please be aware that the likelihood of only 1 out of every

100 individuals purchasing your product or service is rather low. If one is able to generate a daily count of 1000 targeted views for their website, it signifies an average potential for generating 10 sales. Upon careful consideration, it becomes apparent that the aforementioned strategies do not appear to be challenging. This necessitates a certain amount of time and a well-structured course of action. Employ these strategies to maximize success with various affiliate marketing programs. You can sustain a lucrative revenue stream and thrive in this industry, a feat not achievable by all marketers.

Additionally, consider the substantial compensation you will receive.

Steps To Attain Super Affiliate Status

The realm of web hosting has experienced unprecedented growth in recent years. The burgeoning of web hosting demand is driven by the influx of companies venturing into the domain and unearthing the manifold advantages it proffers. It appears to be a prevailing phenomenon in current times.

In the year 2005, a total of 38 million individuals initiated the process of launching their initial website. In the forthcoming year of 2008, it is anticipated that the internet sales sector will outperform the dollar bank. I believe that the majority of these websites provide a wide range of affiliate programs that individuals can select and enlist in. It signifies a sole and singular meaning. Presently, it has become more convenient to locate the most suitable web hosting provider for your application. Seek out prospects within innovative web hosting companies that distinguish themselves from the remaining players in the industry. Subsequently, it is the inadequately skilled individual, rather than the proficient one, who experiences negative consequences. The provision of exemplary customer support is a significant factor to be taken into account when selecting a web hosting service.

It is evident that the efficacy of traditional advertising has diminished Numerous individuals tend to select a web hosting provider on the basis of their visual and auditory impressions. It is additionally founded upon endorsements from individuals who have experienced and achieved favorable outcomes. This presents a significant opportunity for both web hosting partners and resellers. With the plethora of web hosting and software options available, the task of finding the most suitable one is no longer an arduous endeavor. What are the key strategies for achieving success as an affiliate marketer within your specific niche by leveraging web hosting services?

Upon reflection, it is evident that individuals or organizations in need of a website must avail the services of a web hosting company for the purpose of hosting said website. At present, a dominant hosting industry does not exist, consequently individuals tend to select their hosts relying on recommendations. Typically, I acquire such information from individuals who have availed themselves of web hosting services. Given the wide-ranging availability of affiliate programs among hosts, they typically gravitate towards the one that aligns most effectively with their needs and preferences. Consider the merchandise you wish to endorse. Allow them to influence the development of your website and ensure their interests align with your own.

If you have been affiliated with the same host for an extended period of time and have not achieved the desired outcomes despite your diligent endeavors, it may be prudent to relinquish this association and seek an alternative host. It is not necessary to possess something in order to become it. Positive changes are anticipated as you gradually emerge from a challenging state of affairs. Try this. If you are experiencing a high level of contentment and satisfaction with your current web hosting provider, consider exploring the possibility of their provision of an affiliate program, which you can duly enroll in. Rather than making a payment, why not consider taking the opposite approach? Compensation is provided to you in exchange for your services, which can be facilitated through the straightforward method of including a small "offer" or "hosted" link on the webpage, thus establishing an affiliation. What is the rationale behind investing in web hosting services if they are unnecessary for your needs? Earn money by promoting your web hosting provider to individuals who appreciate their service. When making a decision regarding a web hosting provider, opt for a company that provides top-notch customer support. In addition, there is a multitude of hosting affiliate programs available. All remaining affiliate programs will be published in due course. It is a program that generates monthly profits by a specific percentage for customers referred to it. This enables you to secure a reliable and consistent stream of revenue. Indeed, unwavering perseverance can result in substantial achievements within this domain. There exist numerous untapped market opportunities that are awaiting suitable partnerships to materialize and achieve their aspirations. Having a clear understanding of the initial steps instills a sense of self-assurance in one's capabilities and the positive outcomes that will be attained. Website hosting is a lucrative affiliate market in which one can endeavor to secure a substantial, sustainable income over a prolonged period. It is imperative to acknowledge that achieving success in the realm of business necessitates a considerable investment of time, diligent effort, and unwavering perseverance. To date, a flawlessly optimized affiliate market remains elusive. However, there are individuals who possess the expertise to significantly expand such a market. It solely hinges upon one's understanding of the market dynamics and strategically capitalizing on them.

The Importance of Contemplating Affiliate Marketing in the Present Day

For individuals involved in affiliate marketing or seeking legitimate methods of online income generation, there exists a highly viable business opportunity that carries substantial financial rewards. Embracing this venture as an affiliate marketer promises numerous advantages and potential growth. Some of which are

❖ ABSENCE OF PRODUCTION COSTS: In the capacity of an affiliate marketer, you are relieved of any burden to bear production costs, as the merchant has already assumed the responsibility for the product's development.

The initial investment required is comparatively lower: as an affiliate marketer, all you need to operate your business efficiently is a reliable internet connection, a functional smartphone, a laptop, and a suitable workspace.

There are no associated fees or licensing costs involved as affiliate programs generally have no joining charges. The extent of your geographic market is proportional to your capacity to promote your website. The internet serves as a global platform for commercial transactions. One can avail oneself of the opportunities presented by this market.

❖ Virtually any item can be sold—There may be a few blog sites that struggle to identify a relevant product to endorse within their specific field, yet their options are restricted. An extensive array of products and services are available for purchase in the online marketplace. There exists a multitude of affiliate programs, thus facilitating the identification of products that are pertinent to either your existing website or the prospective website you intend to establish.

❖ Remote work is possible: as an affiliate marketer, you have the advantage of choosing your own work location, allowing you to conduct your business activities efficiently from the convenience of your own residence, while still generating income. Additionally, this affords you abundant opportunities to engage in meaningful interactions with your loved ones, while concurrently alleviating the strain of rushing to work early and returning home late on a daily basis.

❖ The risk involved is minimal—Should the sale of a product prove unprofitable, one can simply cease its marketing and explore alternative options. It is imperative that you remove your associated hyperlinks and engage in the promotion of an alternative product. It's that simple. There is no need for you to be concerned about being caught in a lengthy contractual agreement that restricts you from endorsing a product that fails to generate sales.

❖ The potential for substantial earnings exists—By establishing your own online affiliate business, your income potential remains unrestricted, dependent solely on your dedication and diligence. Admittedly, not everyone earns a substantial income. You must demonstrate a willingness to exert diligent endeavor, ensuring the search, establishment, and advertisement of the products. If you effectively market your products and generate substantial traffic to your website, you can establish a thriving affiliate enterprise.

If you possess a personal computer, you are enabled to engage in work remotely from any location across the globe. Have you ever nurtured the desire to embark on a journey, only to be hindered by the unavailability of leave from professional obligations? Should this be the case, affiliate marketing would be an ideal choice. You carry your workplace wherever you go. You would be able to manage your work within a few hours each day, affording you the freedom to travel to any destination of your choice and continue your professional obligations.

WHAT IS THIS?

This constitutes an exceedingly uncomplicated approach to endorse affiliate offers through the direct reproduction and placement of advertisements.

Rest assured, I shall provide you a comprehensive and transparent demonstration of our operations without omitting any details.

Prior to delving into the topic at hand, may I first introduce myself and establish the rationale for your attention towards my insights?

Greetings, ladies and gentlemen. I am Alvaro Gutierrez, and I have been earning an income through digital means for the past eight years, utilizing my laptop as my primary work tool. I am fortunate to have two wonderful children, who happen to be twins—a daughter and a son—as well as a spouse who is exceptionally dear to me.

However, my journey commenced in the year 2000...

In the year 2000, I was employed in an automotive manufacturing facility located in the United Kingdom, diligently engaged for seven consecutive days each week. This commitment to work schedule was a personal decision of mine. Despite the physically demanding nature of the work, life was highly satisfying as I received a handsome remuneration and had the serendipitous opportunity to encounter my now-spouse. I was fully occupied with my professional commitments, diligently allocating my resources towards the attainment of my residence, which I ultimately purchased after a span of one year.

During that period, I commenced a supplementary venture involving the establishment of a Network Marketing enterprise. However, I must confess that I did not excel in this endeavor. Perhaps my Spanish accent played a role in my underperformance (or at least that is the rationale I choose to attribute it to, humorously speaking).

However, in 2007, I came to the realization that I had expended a substantial amount of both financial resources and time on my supplementary occupation, yet had very little to show for it. Subsequently, I transitioned into an office-based role for the ensuing five years, only to eventually be terminated from my employment. It appears that my personal disposition got the better of me, as I exhibited rudeness towards a customer, an attitude that is undoubtedly no longer acceptable in today's professional climate. Mrs. Green, if you happen to be perusing this message, please accept my sincerest apologies.

In any case or in any event, the ultimate outcome is that I became unemployed. However, at that point, I had the responsibility of caring for my two-month-old infants and was devoid of any source of income.

To summarize concisely, I embarked on drop-shipping through the eBay platform. Remarkably, within the span of my initial month, I achieved a noteworthy profit exceeding £900 (approximately $1200). Admittedly, this accomplishment was not without sacrifice, as I dedicated arduous 18-hour days, neglecting even precious moments with my children. The motivation driving my relentless efforts stemmed from the dire circumstance of ensuring basic sustenance for my family.

Presently, I find myself incapable – despite my extensive expertise – of reproducing those outcomes... the market has undergone an overwhelming level of saturation, and eBay has introduced significant obstacles for newcomers attempting to enter the field... There is a conspicuous abundance of young individuals on the platform of Youtube who espouse certain ways of life, yet it is evident that a substantial majority among them lack genuine understanding and expertise, merely instructing on theoretical principles. It is not an insurmountable challenge, but rather a highly arduous task.

In the year 2015, my business experienced significant disruption due to the actions taken by Paypal, resulting in substantial financial losses. They began withholding a substantial amount of funds, which were the product of my diligent efforts. Evidently, Paypal deemed my business operations to be excessively successful, thus categorizing me as a risk to their interests.

Suddenly, an amount totaling approximately £5000 was unexpectedly withheld for a duration of six months, if my recollection serves me correctly. This sum constituted the funds I required to cover both my living expenses and eBay fees. Soon I was unable to pay eBay fees and eventually lost my business as I could no longer keep selling in their platform until the fees were paid.

The situation became incredibly dire, to the point where we were on the verge of homelessness. Our housing lease agreement concluded, leaving us with insufficient funds to secure alternative accommodations. Additionally, as my primary source of income was derived from online sales, I lacked the necessary documentation to substantiate my income to rental agencies. BIG MESS.

In conclusion, we eventually found ourselves residing in my parents' exceedingly compact apartment, where we resided on the sofa for a duration of 1 year. This arrangement involved the cohabitation of 6 individuals in a living space spanning approximately 50 square meters, resulting in quite limited quarters. Transporting the children to their school, located at an approximate distance of one hour from our residence, through the utilization of public transportation. I spend a total of four hours per day solely on commuting to and from school. Nightmare.

Following that year, I successfully revived my business with the support of a generous friend who graciously provided me with a loan of £3000 to cover my outstanding eBay fees, thereby enabling me to resume operations. Thank YOU. You are well aware of your identity.

I acquired valuable insights through a challenging experience... encountering considerable difficulties that encompassed not only financial aspects but also had profound effects on my mental, physical, and spiritual well-being.

However, despite the aforementioned obstacles, I eventually regained control of my business. Since that pivotal moment, I have consistently employed the same strategies with remarkable financial success. These strategies have not only proven effective in the realm of ecommerce, but also in various other social media platforms. Nonetheless, it is important to note that I have modified my approach over time.

Furthermore, it is pleasing to report that...

Presently, should you possess genuine determination to enhance your life, I am also equipped to extend my assistance...

If you are prepared, we may commence.

Chapter Two: Ideal Client

I have been consistently exposed to this notion on numerous occasions from various marketing professionals concerning the ideal target clientele.

Alternatively, understanding your niche: what is its significance?

This is because by catering exclusively to a particular group of customers, you will be better positioned to meet their specific needs and requirements.

Given that they possess similar sets of requirements. Thus, your assistance will be within reach.

Enabling them to attain success, which in turn would prove beneficial for your enterprise.

Please see around you. Do all bloggers possess identical requisites or not?

Do all affiliate marketers selling the same product possess identical requirements or is there variation among them?

You will discover that indeed, they possess identical prerequisites. This is the reason why it is imperative to be aware

your dream customer .

Where Is Your Customer

This concept was introduced to me for the first time through a book authored by an exceedingly renowned marketer.

Once again, the expertise of an organic traffic specialist has reminded me of that particular concept.

Subsequently, I came to realize the tremendous potency of this concept.

If you are aware of the preferred locations frequented by your ideal clientele, at what times are they typically present?

Subsequently, it will be highly feasible for you to secure this client.

You should identify the online platforms where your customer base frequently gathers.

But where ? The solution is quite straightforward; the answer is groups.

All Social Media Groups consist of a certain number of individuals.

You simply need to engage with relevant organizations.

For instance, if your ideal customer is from the CA region, you may want to explore groups that are specifically associated with CA.

Alternatively, you may navigate to the Search bar and input "Chartered Accountants" before pressing the Enter key.

then select Groups. Kindly consider joining the groups and expressing your gratitude to the administrator by posting a thank-you message.

We would like to inform you that your post will either be approved immediately or will be subject to approval.

If granted approval, you will be able to derive further advantages from this.

Please be mindful that not all groups have a preference for content sharing.

Now you have successfully approached your desired customer.

Chapter 1: Analysis of Niche

In advance of progressing our business, it is imperative that we ascertain the specific market segment we are targeting. A niche denotes a market that is characterized by a narrow scope, thereby resulting in diminished competition and increased prospects for success. As acknowledged by some marketers, it is generally more advantageous to hold a prominent position in a confined or niche environment rather than having a lesser influence in a vast and competitive setting.

As an initial step, we suggest that you engage in a process of ideation to compile a comprehensive roster of:

Your hobbies.

Your interests.

Your passions.

If you have any antecedent conceptions in terms of business ventures or product innovations.

The objective is to contemplate prospective offerings or a specific market segment upon which we can establish our business. By amalgamating entrepreneurship with a personal hobby or passion, one can acquire a substantial competitive edge. Engaging in tasks that align with your interests will significantly enhance your enthusiasm for content creation, marketing, and other relevant undertakings. Allow yourself ample time for this stage and thoroughly explore every idea. For instance, if one has a fondness for men's fashion, a more specific focus could be directed towards the realm of fashion catering to larger-bodied individuals.

Tools

Indeed, your explorations within the niche realm extend far beyond the confines of your own cerebral faculties. We have access to a wide range of complimentary resources that can assist us in identifying lucrative markets.

Amazon & eBay

One of the myriad of sources that marketers avail themselves of to seek inspiration for products and niches is the list of Amazon's Best Sellers.

Amazon graciously presents a comprehensive selection of the most popular products in each respective category. Peruse different categories and make observations regarding the current popularity of products. Please bear in mind that our current objective is to accumulate an extensive range of niche product concepts. Additionally, Ebay provides a comparable service that divulges the categories that are highly sought after. Please peruse the top-selling products and their corresponding prices.

Google Trends

Google provides a plethora of exceptional resources for business owners, among which is Google Trends. This feature enables users to access real-time insights on the most trending topics and corresponding search data. Utilize this resource to generate innovative product ideas and engage in brainstorming sessions pertaining to subjects of interest.

Moreover, Google Trends can serve as a valuable tool for validating niche markets and product ideas, particularly those that you already have in mind. Upon entering a search term of your choice, a graph depicting its popularity over a range of several years will be presented.

In relation to the aforementioned graph, the query "Hoverboard" was entered into the search engine. These products were briefly in vogue, garnering substantial attention in recent times, yet their popularity has swiftly waned. This can be readily observed through the prominent increase witnessed throughout the years 2015 and 2016. The graph below exhibits the distribution of interest by region, with the option to toggle between country and city visibility.

Upon entering a keyword in Google Trends, it is essential to thoroughly analyze the associated graph. It is advisable to refrain from engaging with products and industries that exhibit the aforementioned characteristics. There is a high likelihood that these are not expected to elicit a favorable response. This is not an absolute certainty, but it serves as a reliable guideline to adhere to. Rather, you should direct your attention towards markets that exhibit enduring or emerging interest.

By utilizing regional information, we obtain insights regarding the origins of searches, thereby yielding general demographic information. Subsequently, presented beneath are the corresponding search durations and subjects.

When conducting term inquiries on Google Trends, it is possible to input several subjects or keywords to facilitate a comparison of their outcomes.

Expanding upon the hoverboard illustration, we introduced two additional comparable items to draw a distinction.

Each distinct hue represents a specific concept that we have inputted. As stated earlier, these products garnered substantial attention, primarily attributed to the endorsements by notable public figures, yet subsequently experienced a rapid decline in their desirability. Please analyze the aforementioned charts in order to draw comparisons and highlight distinctions among products, concepts, and market segments.

Trend Websites

Producthunt.com is among a multitude of websites that diligently track emerging products across diverse markets. The items that garner the highest level of popularity are exhibited regularly, both on a daily and weekly basis. Examine their various categories and make a record of those that capture your interest.

At present, http://trendhunter.com stands as the preeminent and widely acclaimed trend community, holding the title for being the largest and most prominent globally. Trend Hunter provides an excellent online platform for entrepreneurs in search of product ideas, given its extensive worldwide community comprising 137,000 members and a broad fan base of 3 million individuals.

Ultimately, http://springwise.com consolidates an abundance of entrepreneurial concepts from across the globe into a singular hub. Each and every geographical location across the globe exhibits distinct operating methodologies and embodies diverse cultural values. Springwise scours the globe to uncover the most exceptional entrepreneurial concepts, narratives, and patterns.

Review Websites

Much like trend websites, review sites can offer ample inspiration and concepts for various products. Regarded as a highly esteemed platform, the website http://uncrate.com is widely recognized for its immense popularity. It effectively features a diverse array of products encompassing categories such as clothing, technology, automobiles, and real estate. They additionally provide case studies that provide a more thorough examination and comprehension. You will encounter an abundance of contemporary and novel concepts from which to derive inspiration.

Google Alerts

An additional valuable resource offered by Google is their alert service. You are able to enter keywords and receive email notifications whenever news related to those keywords is published. Staying current with your industry is crucial for discerning emerging trends and potential prospects.

Enclosing keywords such as "digital marketing" within quotation marks will yield distinct search outcomes. Omitting the use of quotation marks when entering the search term will yield more comprehensive news results. Prioritize the inclusion of the tilde symbol (~) preceding the designated keyword, such as ~digital marketing, when searching for synonymous terms. This will additionally serve as a notification to draw your attention.

If you have transitioned into this unit, it is expected that you have identified a specific market segment or specialized area that you intend to pursue. We firmly assert that market research ought not to be excessively challenging or comprehensive. It would be more appropriate to view it as a chance to acquire knowledge and make necessary preparations for the future. "It is an obligatory practice within the domain of entrepreneurship and affords numerous advantages, namely:

Improving the effectiveness of communication with your customers. Gaining insight into the preferences, behavior patterns, and related details of your target demographic enables you to customize your marketing strategies accordingly. Understanding their preferences and expectations is crucial for effectively communicating in their language, so to speak.

Identify opportunities. Engaging in market research can provide valuable insights into the industry, enabling the identification of potential opportunities that can be capitalized upon. You have the opportunity to leverage a product that is not offered by the competition, enabling you to potentially exploit it for your advantage.

Minimize risks. Through a comprehensive understanding of the target market, you will be able to ascertain the level of competition present, identify prevailing trends, and steer clear of potential pitfalls.

Competitive intelligence. By comprehending the methods of promotion, positioning, and marketing strategy execution employed by your competitors, you can derive valuable insights to adapt and enhance your own plans.

Identify problems. During the process of devising your website and marketing strategy, you will have the opportunity to identify any prospective challenges that may arise. Furthermore, you will have the capability to discern consumer issues and develop innovative solutions accordingly.

Competitive Analysis

Commence by accessing the Google search engine and entering a relevant keyword pertaining to your particular domain. Building upon the aforementioned illustration regarding merchandise associated with men's tennis, we shall now make reference to the outcomes pertaining to the category of "men's tennis equipment." With a substantial 1.3 million search results, it is evident that there exists a respectable level of competition, yet it does not reach the point of overwhelming saturation. Let us delve into these websites further and inquire ourselves the following queries:

How are they providing value?

Which social media platforms are they utilizing?

What is the structural design of the website? (Minimalistic, resembling a blog format, etc.)

What types of content do they utilize? (Infographics, articles, etc)

Are there opportunities present? What actions can I take that they are not currently undertaking?

It is crucial to analyze this information as it can subsequently be incorporated into our website in the foreseeable future. Please ensure that you diligently observe and take note of any discernible trends and patterns that may arise during the analysis of the stores. It is prudent to examine prosperous companies and implement comparable marketing strategies. Presented below is an instance of conducting a thorough analysis of rival websites in order to glean innovative concepts and strategies.

Forums

A prime location for accessing a narrow market segment is in the midst of discussions being held by individuals regarding the subject matter. Please proceed to Google's website and enter a relevant keyword followed by the terms "forum" or "discussion board" in the search bar. This will present outcomes pertaining to numerous forums within your specific industry. This is a straightforward approach that holds significant potency, given our direct engagement with the consumer. Peruse the boards and contemplate the following inquiries:

What aspects of the product do they appreciate?

What alterations would they prefer to observe?

Can you provide information regarding the demographic characteristics of these individuals?

Forums occasionally host discussions pertaining to professions, education, and related subjects. These discussions are ideal for establishing a more profound comprehension of your target demographic. Record comprehensive information pertaining to their demographic attributes, including but not limited to their average age range, income level, and areas of interest.

Social Media

Social media has the potential to serve not only as a tool for demographic research, but also as a means for conducting competitive analysis. Conduct a thorough examination of influential individuals operating within your target market on social media platforms such as Facebook, Twitter, and Instagram. Analyze the methods employed by the company to establish their brand, promote their content, ascertain the composition of their posts, and extract relevant details. Subsequently, you can employ these analogous strategies in the event that your social media accounts are functional.

To gain a deeper understanding of the consumer, investigate social channels using a similar approach. Determine the manner in which the audience communicates their opinions and feedback regarding the services and products. Once you understand their desires and requirements, it becomes possible to create tailored product descriptions, blog posts, advertisements, and similar content that aligns with their preferences and expectations.

What Are The Qualities Of An Effective Affiliate Program?

Recurring revenue reigns supreme

What is the underlying cause behind the majority of individuals persisting in employment that brings them discontentment?

The stability of a reliable income source is the "security" being referred to.

In reality, there exists a rather limited sense of stability and assurance when one chooses to engage in employment under another individual or organization, for the possibility of being terminated, experiencing a reduction in workforce, or witnessing business insolvency remains ever present. I have recently undergone a situation where I was unexpectedly terminated from my supposedly stable employment. You are assuming a level of risk regardless of the course of action you choose; therefore, it would be prudent to strive for what you desire.

But the dependability of a recurring paycheck is an enticing thing.

Hence, it is recommended to endeavor to replicate a comparable system or process within your own organization. It may appear implausible to achieve this with endeavors such as affiliate marketing; nonetheless, it must be acknowledged that the potential for continuous revenue does indeed exist. All you need to do is identify the suitable program.

An example. The affiliate program provided by ClickFunnels offers ongoing commissions for every sale made of their software used for building funnels. The percentage varies between 20% and 40%.

What does this mean?

This entails that upon successfully referring someone to register for ClickFunnels using your affiliate link, you will receive a recurring commission of 20% - 40% for every subsequent month in which the individual continues to pay their subscription fee. That pertains to the single instance when you successfully closed the deal.

They are associated with your profile and account, and ClickFunnels expresses profound gratitude by consistently compensating you a proportional share of the monthly subscription fee.

Imagine the scenario wherein you establish a clientele base consisting of precisely one hundred individuals, each of whom contributes a monthly sum ranging from $97 to $297. The monthly amount for automatic recurring payments ranges from $1,940 to $11,880. Certainly, it is necessary to address the issue of churn rate, which pertains to individuals terminating their accounts. However, this is precisely why implementing effective mechanisms to continually attract new clientele becomes imperative.

Once a substantial and stable stream of recurring income has been established, sufficient to sustain one's current standard of living, a considerable amount of time is liberated, affording the opportunity to focus on projects of personal interest and devise strategic approaches for advancing one's business to a higher echelon.

You have effectively substituted or even amplified your previous salary, thereby granting you a life unrestricted by financial constraints.

It is essential to acknowledge that not all of your income will be of a recurring nature. There exist commendable affiliate programs that do not require you to pay a monthly fee in exchange for a single sale. In order for these programs to be effective, it is necessary to establish robust and proficient systems, as each sale commission marks the culmination of the transaction. You are now tasked with the responsibility of seeking a completely new individual who possesses the desire to invest their funds in the product/service you are promoting.

That presents a significantly greater level of difficulty compared to securing a single sale and subsequently receiving continuous commission for an extended period.

This is precisely why consistent revenue holds a position of utmost importance. It is highly advisable to explore the option of securing a recurring revenue affiliate program as the fundamental framework of your business endeavor, which would facilitate the replacement of your regular income source while simultaneously affording you greater freedom and flexibility with your time.

Alternatively, if you do not change your approach, you will find yourself perpetually striving for increased sales, effectively reverting to a laborer who is obliged to exchange time for remuneration.

Commission Rates

Commission rates significantly influence the program deserving of your valuable time for promotion. The following figures represent the proportions of the sales revenue that you will receive for generating traffic, and subsequently facilitating sales, to the company's website.

It is imperative to bear in mind that there exists a disparity among affiliate programs, and we seek a scheme that justly remunerates us for the dedicated time and effort invested.

In addition, it is imperative that we take into account the commission rates, along with the sale price and frequency. The percentage alone doesn't determine if the program is a good one.

Given that the commission rate is just 10%, the potential to earn $500 per sale on a $5,000 product makes it viable to direct efforts towards promoting this offer and driving sales.

On the other hand, in the event that we are receiving commissions of 40% on a product priced at $10, it will be necessary for us to generate an exorbitant volume of traffic in order to sustain a livelihood, as we are only earning $4 per sale. Simple math.

Several affiliate programs available have a confluence of unfavorable commission rates and sale prices. Certain items on the Amazon platform yield a commission rate of merely 4% given a product value of $12. This scenario presents a combination of unfavorable circumstances, and it is highly improbable that any form of traffic will generate substantial wealth through $0.48 commissions.

As previously stated, we also wish to take into account the frequency of your commissions. If you are receiving a commission rate of 20% on a product priced at $97, and considering that the payment is recurrent on a monthly basis, it may be advantageous to consider pursuing this opportunity. This is because each sale will contribute $19.40 to your monthly recurring revenue. While it may appear inconsequential at first glance, the cumulative effect of erecting 100 of these units would yield a monthly passive income of $1,940.

Conducting a thorough examination of the mathematics involved and comprehending the potential outcomes of an affiliate program prior to enrolling constitutes a critical undertaking. You would not wish to expend a significant amount of your time or financial resources on a program only to discover that it is an unfavorable venture with limited returns. That is an expeditious route to exhaustion and downfall.

The optimum affiliate agreement consists of a substantial commission rate, a significant sales price, and a recurring payment schedule. Software as a service (SaaS) is typically a favorable industry to explore, as it frequently presents opportunities of this nature available for promotional purposes.

Cookies

It is now appropriate to discuss the topic of cookies.

No, not those cookies; although they are enjoyable to snack on while composing written material.

In the context of affiliate marketing, the term "cookies" pertains to a code segment that becomes associated with a visitor's browser subsequent to their engagement with your hyperlink.

This code serves as a means to notify the affiliate program that the site visit is attributed to your content, thus entitling you to proper acknowledgment for the sale and subsequent commission payment.

The issue associated with cookies is their tendency to reach their expiration date. The typical lifespan of a cookie varies from one day to sixty days on average, and in some cases can extend beyond 365 days.

Fundamentally, this expiration is affording you the advantage of being presumed innocent or given the benefit of any doubts. If an individual is presented with an offer and proceeds to click on your link without making a purchase on the same day, the extended duration of the cookie ensures that all optimism is not completely lost.

On the other hand, in the event that the individual reverts back to the offer during the duration of the cookie's existence and proceeds with a purchase, you will continue to receive acknowledgment for having presented said offer to said person.

Amazon serves as another illustrative instance of an inadequate program for this purpose. Due to the substantial volume of visitors that Amazon attracts and its extensive reputation, the company merely offers a 24-hour cookie duration. This implies that in the event that a day passes following the clicking of your Amazon Affiliate link, Amazon assumes that any subsequent purchase made by the individual is unrelated to the original link, resulting in the forfeiture of your credit. The primary reason for my limited promotion of Amazon products is the combination of low commissions and a brief tracking duration for cookies.

Conversely, obscure startups lack the widespread recognition that Amazon enjoys. A software such as Funnelytics might offer a cookie duration of 365 days, as it is improbable that the customer was exposed to their brand through any other means within that timeframe.

Programs that offer extended cookie durations are advantageous and generally result in higher sale prices, as they accommodate the fact that individuals may require more time to deliberate and finalize their purchase decisions.

Another important aspect to consider when it comes to cookies is the distinction between first-click and... last-click.

Upon the initial click, the affiliate whose link was first clicked shall be credited with the sale, irrespective of whether they subsequently click on affiliate links from other affiliates within the designated period of the cookie window.

With the utilization of last-click attribution, in the event that an individual selects your hyperlink, yet subsequently clicks on a different affiliate's hyperlink within the designated cookie timeframe, your accreditation will be forfeited.

Please ensure that you have a clear understanding of the specific category of credit that is designated for your program.

Your Stock Mix

Although this publication does not specifically deal with personal finance, it is my sincere wish that through reading it, your financial situation experiences improvement.

In the present context, when discussing a combination of stocks, it represents a particular mentality or outlook.

In the realm of stock investment, it is widely acknowledged that dispersing funds across multiple stocks is a prudent strategy, discouraging the concentration of wealth in a singular or limited set of stocks. To effectively manage and minimize your risk exposure, it is advisable to diversify your investments by allocating resources across a range of companies spanning various industries. This arrangement ensures that in the event of a downturn or negative performance by a specific company or sector, your entire investment portfolio is not subjected to complete loss.

Maintain this perspective while collaborating with affiliate programs. Initially, it is advisable to exert substantial effort towards a singular program that aligns with your fervor, boasts a lucrative compensation, and in which you possess adept selling skills. However, relying solely on the influx of automatic commissions should not constitute your exclusive source of income.

Bad things can happen.

What would happen in the event of the company's insolvency? In the event that they determine they are capable of independently marketing their products and choose to terminate their affiliate program, what would be the implications? What would be the implications if they were to initiate reductions in commission percentages or if you were to inadvertently contravene an unrecognized rule, potentially resulting in expulsion from the program?

There is a multitude of undesirable outcomes that could transpire if one were to place all their eggs in a single basket. Hence, it is crucial to expand and vary your options once you have secured a favorable offer.

When the launch of Traffic Secrets occurred in March 2020, I discovered an effective means of consistently generating substantial commissions. This entailed that I possessed a moderately dependable source of revenue for my enterprise.

Although it was advantageous to finally find a successful solution, I recognized the potential for fluctuation and consequently persevered in promoting alternative affiliate offers. Smaller offers, such as Noom, which yield a payment of merely $15 - $20 per trial signup, have effectively contributed to generating supplementary income for my business.

In order to diversify and cater to a wide range of potential customers, I am inclined towards incorporating a blend of affordable and premium offerings, while also including offerings from individual companies such as ClickFunnels, as well as from established marketplaces like Impact Radius or Brandcycle.

This enables me to effectively manage risk from all perspectives and ensure that in the event of a marketplace or company's decline, my business remains unaffected.

My utmost recommendation is to fully commit to a single affiliate program until you achieve seamless automation, subsequently redirecting your resources towards expanding your business by successfully establishing and enhancing additional programs. By adopting this approach, you will establish valuable resources (such as content, software, and personnel) for your enterprise through automated financial transactions, thereby expanding to a level where your business is no longer dependent on a singular vulnerable element.

I find it inconceivable to exert such immense effort, forego valuable time with my loved ones and recreational pursuits, only to have my business perilously reliant on a singular component, consequently risking the loss of everything solely due to another individual's behavior.

Indeed, I possess the capability to do so, as I have personally experienced it. However, a more detailed discussion on this matter will be provided later.

Advocate for your passions.

An exemplary affiliate program is characterized by your enthusiasm in promoting it.

If one harbors strong aversion towards the product, its concept, or its underlying values, not only will this result in personal dissatisfaction with one's work, but it will also become evident through one's demeanor, consequently deterring potential customers from making purchases.

It is probable that you will also possess strong moral objections towards engaging in the sale of a product or service that you hold in disdain, and it is likely that you will involuntarily undermine your own progress at a subconscious level, thereby impeding your path to achieving success. Optimal commission rates hold lesser significance if one harbors discomfort towards the product.

Ensure that you are endorsing and advocating for the things that you possess genuine affection for.

An approach to initiate the process of finding an affiliate program involves conducting a comprehensive search for brands and themes that resonate profoundly with your personal preferences and interests.

It may come as a surprise to learn that a significant number of companies have implemented affiliate programs. Please refer to the bottom menu, specifically the footer, on their website where you will find a section labeled "Affiliates" or "Partners". You should have the capability to navigate to, peruse, and submit an application for their program using that platform.

The company ought to include the program's specifications (such as cookie length and commission rate) on the application page, enabling you to make an informed assessment of its suitability prior to submitting an application.

Kindly consider the brands that you utilize regularly, weekly, or monthly. Carefully consider your areas of expertise or personal interests, and then seek out brands that align with those particular domains.

At some juncture, it is probable that you will come across an affiliate marketing marketplace (which will be further discussed in the subsequent chapter), wherein you have the opportunity to discover analogous brands for promotional purposes.

Engaging in affiliate marketing offers an enjoyable experience, yet it can also entail periods of arduous effort. Furthermore, without a deep-rooted passion for the promoted product, overcoming these challenging periods can prove to be formidable.

Stay Focused

It appears that maintaining concentration conflicts with the previously provided recommendation on the allocation of stocks, isn't that correct?

While it is advantageous to possess a range of offers to endorse, it is not advisable to indiscriminately endorse every single opportunity that presents itself. As you commence the development of your blog, video channel, podcast, or any other medium through which you choose to promote products, you will inevitably begin to garner an audience. They will locate you and reach out to you in order to enlist your support in marketing their product.

Occasionally, they may provide complimentary products or grant access to software/applications as an incentive for you to generate content about their offerings. Others will offer cash. While the allure of these offers may be enticing, it is advisable to only consider those that align harmoniously with your messaging and theme for optimal results.

Determine the target audience and desired means of communication, and adhere strictly to these parameters without any deviation. It can get expensive.

Initially, upon commencing my pursuit of acquiring lifetime software deals, I would frequently procure a plethora of novel offerings featured on AppSumo. This proclivity arose from envisioning their potential utilization within my enterprise at a later point in time.

The issue pertained to the lack of alignment between these programs and my mission or objectives at that particular moment in time. Consequently, a substantial amount of funds is currently tied up in these unused programs, resulting from a lofty notion that I may potentially execute in the future.

While proactive strategic planning is highly recommended, deviating from the intended course will deplete the financial resources of your enterprise. I am currently encountering a program that appears intriguing; however, I exercise caution in purchasing it. I am inclined to retain funds within my business, allocating them towards endeavors that will genuinely contribute to its expansion.

We receive inquiries from various companies seeking the opportunity to engage our audience through promotional efforts. However, if their offerings do not align with our interests and values, we politely decline. The allocation of time is inherently limited, surpassing even the constraints placed on financial resources.

Ensure that your portfolio composition and expenditures align with the core principles of your messaging and business mission, maintain steadfastness in your pursuits, and diligently persevere. It has been suggested that focusing on a narrow scope and achieving great depth is the most effective approach. Stick to it.

Efficient Methods for Searching for a Product

Initially, I encountered considerable difficulty in determining which product to endorse. There is considerable discourse surrounding the selection of a niche, primarily driven by its impact on search engine optimization (SEO). However, an intriguing question arises: what specific niche should one opt for?

One experiences apprehension regarding the selection of a niche that may lack interest among others, fail to generate sufficient revenue, or present challenges in terms of ranking. Moreover, one tends to engage in excessive contemplation, leading to the consequent proliferation of complications and a sense of fear. When anxiety reaches its peak, it is imperative to halt.

You must cease and temporarily set aside all of your emotions. It is imperative that you engage your cognitive faculties in a rational manner.

The one who possesses an affinity for numerals and precise standards.

General criteria

To enhance the likelihood of success in your business, certain specific criteria must be met by a product. The aforementioned criteria are directly associated with the extent of consumer interest in the product, as well as the volume of online platforms that discuss it.

As a novice, it will be important for you to identify products that exhibit a substantial level of search activity, alongside a moderate degree of competition. You will be provided with instructions on locating this information without charge in the upcoming sections.

An advice

Prior to commencing our task, it is imperative that you maintain a rational mindset until the conclusion of this chapter. Exercise caution in the selection of a product or niche (even in your thoughts) while you are still in the process of elimination.

Cease any contemplation regarding the manner in which you may advertise and promote a commodity. What types of titles or product descriptions could be employed, as well as the design of your website, ... It is premature, and there is a possibility of your disappointment.

Potential consequences of hastily selecting a product:

- You anticipate a significant search volume for a product, yet it manifests as low, and vice versa.

- Although there is a considerable volume of searches with limited competition, a prominent website already dominates the first pages of Google search results. Although it remains an option to pursue that particular product, it would entail a substantial amount of effort to achieve visibility on the first or second page.

Find your product

1- Employ the use of an Incognito window

In order to gain access to the most authentic data, it is necessary to open Amazon using a secure and private browsing session. Alternatively, in lieu of discovering individuals' desired search results, one may receive product recommendations tailored to their personal attributes such as age, geographical location, search history, and an extensive range of additional data points the system possesses concerning individuals.

In order to ensure the highest level of accuracy in the information you receive, it is recommended that you consider deleting your cookies and utilizing a web browser that prioritizes user privacy, such as Brave or Opera. Nevertheless, it is not obligatory, and utilizing the private browsing mode should suffice.

2- Utilize the search function to ascertain the queries and interests of users.

Next:

1. You are required to input a letter into the search bar and allow it to generate suggestions based on popular user queries.

2. Capture a screenshot of the content and employ an optical character recognition (OCR) tool to extract the information as text. Afterwards, transfer the list onto a sheet or table, and proceed to replicate this procedure for each letter of the alphabet.

In order to obtain precise findings regarding the search behavior of prospective users, it is imperative to employ the alphabet that they utilize.

3- Analyze the keywords

We intend to utilize Google's Keyword Planner to conduct an analysis of the list of keywords you have obtained. This tool is provided at no cost and is an authorized service. However, to utilize it, it is necessary to establish an account and set up a campaign beforehand. By undertaking this action, you will be granted unrestricted usage of the tool whenever necessary.

Utilize the sorting method to extract the keywords that fulfill the predefined criteria, thereafter compiling them into a comprehensive list.

4- Analyze the competition

Please ensure that you examine the competition for each product listed.

To accomplish this, ascertain the individuals or entities that appear on the initial page of Google's search results. Are there known companies/websites? Are there niche websites? Are there online platforms that, despite employing identical keywords, do not exclusively offer the same merchandise?

Please conduct an analysis of the initial three pages and record your observations and interpretations of those pages. Are they well done? Complete? Slow?

Record all pertinent information for the purpose of making an informed decision regarding the subsequent course of action.

5- It is now time to select the victor.

After conducting thorough research, it is necessary to eliminate products that face excessive competition or those where competition is significant.

By engaging in such actions, you will continue to possess only a limited range of 2 or 3 products or niches.

Now is the opportune moment to regain control of your emotions. Select the product that offers a more satisfactory tactile experience for you. The option in which you possess the highest level of expertise, or alternatively, the option that aligns with your purchase preference.

Now that you have selected your product, let us proceed to the next stage.

Techniques for Crafting Social Media Posts and Written Content

Introduction

When commencing a blog, a paramount concern is determining the subject matter to be addressed. With the implementation of Affiliate Marketing, the task becomes increasingly challenging as it necessitates the composition of descriptions pertaining to one's merchandise. Therefore, it is necessary to produce multiple units of content pertaining to the identical category of product.

Furthermore, it should be acknowledged that not all individuals possess the skill of crafting a post. In my personal case, I have always been an avid reader, and during my childhood, I extensively engaged in the art of writing. mainly fiction.

Could you please clarify how one should compose a written piece with the aim of promoting and selling a product? Indeed, this style of writing is commonly referred to as Copywriting. It is a form of written communication that amplifies the product's qualities while effectively engaging with the client. It does not pertain to merely delineating the qualities of a product, but rather elucidating to the potential buyer the reasons why they should consider making a purchase (preferably through your provided link).

It is a straightforward task to compose posts. It is imperative that you acquire knowledge of the method, as it becomes automatic with practice. But, how about SEO? What is the process for implementing SEO strategies in order to enhance the positioning of your posts?

In the forthcoming chapter, we shall commence by exploring the process of conducting SEO research.

Subsequently, we shall observe the possibilities for composing posts in the context of Affiliate Marketing.

Finally, we will learn about copywriting and how to apply it when writing the titles and the meta descriptions of our posts.

Selecting Suitable Affiliate Programs: A Guide To Making An Informed Choice

Prior to enrolling in an affiliate program, it is advisable to inquire first. Conduct a preliminary investigation regarding the decisions made by the program you intend to enroll in. Identify several resolutions as they will serve as the definitive indication of your future achievements.

Is there any membership fee associated with joining? The majority of the proposed projects available today are entirely free of charge. Why would you choose to compromise for establishments that require payment before you can become a member?

At what time are the commission checks distributed? Each program is unique. Certain matters arise on a monthly basis, quarterly, and according to similar intervals. Choose the option that aligns with your preferred installment schedule. Several subordinate projects are establishing a minimum commission threshold that a partner must achieve or exceed in order to receive their payments.

What is the ratio of hits to deals? Based on all the partner metrics, this is the average number of interactions with pennants or text links required to generate a successful transaction. This aspect is of utmost significance due to its ability to determine the amount of traffic that needs to be generated in order to achieve a commission from the sale.

How are references originating from a subsidiary's website tracked and what is the duration of their retention within the system? It is imperative that you demonstrate a high degree of certainty regarding the program, to the extent of diligently tracking the individuals to whom you make reference on your website. This represents the primary method through which you can attribute the recognition for a transaction. The duration for which those individuals remain within the framework is also of great significance. This is due to the fact that certain visitors refrain from initial purchase but may later express their intention to procure the product. Determine if you will receive recognition for the transaction regardless of whether it is completed several months after a specified date.

What types of available partner information are there? Your selection of the associate program should be capable of providing comprehensive information. They should be easily accessible online at your convenience.
Regularly monitoring your personal information is fundamental in order to ascertain the current count of impressions, hits, and deals generated from your website. Impressions refer to the instances in which a visitor of your website observed the banner or textual interface. A successful occurrence is determined when an individual taps on

the designated flag or text to become part of a larger entity.

Moreover, does the affiliate program offer compensation for the number of clicks and impressions generated, in addition to the commissions earned from completed transactions? It is essential that impressions and hits are duly compensated, as this will contribute to the revenue derived from sales commissions. This holds particular significance if the program you are enrolled in provides competitive pricing in order to attain a favorable ratio.

May I inquire about the identity of the web-based retailer? Identify the individuals with whom you are collaborating in order to ascertain the credibility of the organization. Familiarize yourself with the products they offer and the average amount they are achieving. The greater your understanding of the retailer's subsidiary program, the easier it will be for you to discern whether that program is genuinely suitable for you and your website.

Does the member belong to a single-tier or dual-tier program? A program operating on an individual level compensates solely for the business that you, as an individual, have generated. A dual-tier program compensates you for the business you generate, in addition to offering you a commission on the sales generated by any affiliate you sponsor in your program. A handful of dual-tier initiatives, regardless, yield minimal costs per each new supporter you endorse. Rather akin to an expenditure incurred in the process of enlisting.

Ultimately, the inquiry pertains to the amount of commission being disbursed. In the majority of projects, the commission paid ranges between 20% and 80%, with some exceptional cases of 100% commission payout. The payment per hit ranges from 0.01% to 0.05%. In the eventuality that you come across a program that offers compensation for impressions as well, the remuneration provided is negligible. Upon examination of the data, you will promptly grasp the rationale behind the significance of the average sales amount and the sales-to-deal ratio.

Prior to enrolling in a membership program, it is essential to address these inquiries, which comprise only a subset of the total set of questions. It is imperative for you to possess comprehensive knowledge regarding the multiple key factors that your selected program should encompass before incorporating them into your website. Make an effort to inquire about these matters regarding your partner's program decisions. These resources can aid you in selecting the appropriate program for your website from the wide array of options available.

Determining Which Networks to Select

There are a plethora of astounding narratives concerning subsidiary initiatives and organizations. Many individuals have become accustomed to hearing these opinions repeatedly, to the extent that some are cautious about aligning themselves with any one viewpoint. The accounts they may have been informed about are those

associated with illicit endeavors or deceptive commercial frameworks. Essentially, this type of market lacks authentic, praiseworthy merchandise.
You would prefer to disassociate yourself from these plans. It is evident that you require a program that provides excellent quality goods which you will readily accept. The increasing count of individuals who have already enrolled and achieved significant success serves as substantial evidence that there exist reputable and high-quality affiliate programs.

What are the advantages of engaging in an affiliate program?

It grants you the opportunity to engage in part-time employment. It provides you with the opportunity to generate a continuous passive income. Additionally, it confers upon you the status of a proprietor of a privately-owned enterprise. Previous subsidiary projects have generated significant wealth for their stakeholders. They embody the tangible evidence of the fruitful outcomes that arise from diligent effort, unwavering dedication to seeking opportunities, and nurturing the growth and development of their peers.

Should you ever decide to proceed with either option, it is imperative that you acknowledge the fact that you are embarking on a venture aligned with your own capabilities and intentions. This will serve as a confirmation that you can achieve success efficiently.

What are the criteria one should consider when selecting a reputable affiliate program for promotion? Before finalizing your selection, please consider the following suggestions for further investigation:

A software application that appeals to you and captivates your interest.

A highly intriguing method to ascertain whether this program aligns with your objectives is by evaluating your own interest in procuring the product. Given the prevailing circumstances, it is highly likely that there exists a considerable number of individuals who share a similar level of interest in said program and its associated products.

Seek out a commendable program that possesses exceptional qualities.

For instance, look for one that has associations with a multitude of experts within that particular sector. In this regard, you can be assured of the program's high quality standards that you will be entering.

Ensure active involvement in those events which provide authentic and viable products.

Do you possess any knowledge or information regarding this matter? Do some underlying examination. If feasible, endeavor to solicit feedback from a selection of individuals and clients regarding the credibility and effectiveness of the program.

The initiative that is providing dedicated attention to a nascent target audience.

This will ensure that an increased and regular number of requests are made for your references. Make requests. There exist social gatherings and dialogues wherein one can actively participate to acquire valuable and reliable feedback.

Selecting a program that offers remuneration in the form of residual pay and a payout exceeding 40% would be an exceptional choice.

There are several initiatives that provide such remuneration. Look carefully for one. Endeavor to avoid investing significant efforts into programs that offer insufficient compensation for your experience.

Take note of the foundational equity stakes that must be fulfilled or consider transactions that are exceedingly challenging to achieve.

Prior to receiving payment, certain prerequisite conditions must be fulfilled for subsidiary projects. It is imperative to ensure that you possess the necessary capabilities to fulfill their requirements.

Please choose an option that offers an extensive range of tools and resources to expedite the growth of your business within the shortest possible timeframe.
Certain partner programs do not possess these limitations. This can lead to your

decision being influenced by numerous helpful tools at your disposal.

Consider the proposition that the program encompasses an established framework, enabling you to thoroughly evaluate your organizations and compensation.

Similarly, ascertain if it is available on the internet for convenient access at your discretion and convenience.

The program excels in providing individuals with ample opportunities for reestablishing their active engagement on each occasion.

The partner program that offers reliable support and advancements to its products has a tendency to retain its members. These factors can ensure the advancement of your organizations.

Acquire knowledge about the concerns that individuals have regarding a program.

Just as with the aforementioned examples, you have the opportunity to conduct your verification during conversational exchanges. If you happen to be acquainted with someone in that analogous program, it would not be remiss to inquire about the potential disadvantages associated with it.

Ensure you possess a thorough understanding of both the subsidiary program and organization you intend to progress within, prioritizing caution and seriousness in this pursuit.

Being aware of the nature of the program you are involved in will enable you to anticipate and prevent any potential challenges that may arise in the future.

How To Initiate The Establishment Of An Affiliate Marketing Enterprise

One can generate commissions via affiliate marketing by promoting and selling the services or products provided by external companies. Affiliate marketing has emerged as a viable and effective means of generating additional income from the comfort of one's own residence. Furthermore, it is relatively effortless to establish affiliations with reputable corporations. Allow me to delineate the procedure for accomplishing this task.

1. Monetize Your Expertise

When embarking on the initial stages, it is advisable to limit oneself to promoting services and products within the realm of one's familiarity and comprehension. In the online marketing community, this practice is commonly referred to as "selecting your specific niche." Seek out a specialized area that pertains to either your professional expertise or personal passions. In essence, focus on identifying a subject matter that is connected to either your occupation or your hobbies and areas of interest.

As an example, if you are engaged in blogging, it is more advantageous to promote and sell books rather than fishing equipment (unless, of course, your blog specifically centers around fishing). Your marketing endeavors are apt to be more fruitful if you direct your attention towards promoting products or services with which you possess a familiarity.

2. Establish an online platform pertinent to your domain

When embarking on an affiliate venture, one's initial step would entail disclosing to prospective companies the specific website through which the products or services would be marketed. This is because the companies must ensure the preservation of their image and reputation, as they are concerned with potential harm caused by the website's content.

Commencing a website is no longer restricted solely to individuals in the professional sphere. Numerous websites, such as WordPress, are available to facilitate the establishment of a personalized online platform for you. Ensure that your website encompasses informative content that is not solely focused on sales. The fundamental objective is for your website to convey an impression of expertise and knowledge in the subject matter.

3. Conduct Research on Affiliate Programs

Do not hastily select the initial affiliate program that comes your way. Seek out a provider that aligns with your specific industry and provides offerings that are directly relevant to your niche.

An alternative option for your consideration is the Amazon program.

Due to its nature as a marketplace, a wide array of products is readily accessible, increasing the likelihood of finding products that cater to your specific niche. The program enjoys substantial popularity and serves as an excellent starting point to venture into the realm of affiliate marketing.

An alternative that you may wish to contemplate is Clickbank. It has gained significant popularity within the community of affiliate marketers. The rationale is straightforward - Clickbank-affiliated companies are renowned for providing highly favorable commission rates.

4. Enroll in an Affiliate Program

Enrolling in an affiliate program typically incurs no fees. It is advisable to exercise caution if a program requests your credit card information solely for the purpose of enrolling you as an affiliate. There is a likelihood that it constitutes fraudulent activity. Reputable corporations do not impose any fees for individuals to join their affiliate programs.

Organizations will request your PayPal or banking details. Don't be alarmed. This simplifies the process to facilitate the payment of your commissions, rather than intended to extract funds from you.

5. Incorporate Affiliate Links within Your Content

One effective approach to generating a commission without gaining a perception solely as a "sales" website is to integrate affiliate links seamlessly within your content. This stimulates individuals to be more inclined towards clicking on the hyperlinks and, naturally, in the event of a purchase, you are entitled to a commission.

As an illustration, consider the scenario where you are in the process of compiling an appraisal concerning a literary work that you have recently perused and found to be enjoyable.

Create a hyperlink out of the book title that directs your visitors to the Amazon website, where they can access the pricing information for the hardcover, softcover, and Kindle editions of the respective book. Readers are subsequently empowered to evaluate and ascertain the most suitable option before making their purchase.

Fortunately, acquiring links to the websites of these companies is a relatively simple process. The methods by which you acquire the links may vary, naturally, though discovering the links to the products you intend to sell is not arduous in the slightest.

6. Ensure to incorporate visual advertisements in the sidebar section

Majority of websites exhibit a sidebar; it is highly likely that yours is no exception. The sidebar provides an excellent opportunity to display visual advertisements related to the products that are featured on your website.

Furthermore, it can be observed that businesses with affiliate programs provide streamlined processes for accessing the links and images that will redirect your visitors to their respective websites. Typically, it suffices to merely duplicate and insert code into the adjacent sidebar.

7. Consistently generate relevant content within your designated industry.

In order to sustain a steady stream of commissions, it is imperative to maintain a consistent flow of visitors to your website. To accomplish this, it is essential to maintain a consistent and frequent update schedule for your website, incorporating pertinent content each time. This practice is commonly referred to by digital marketers as "content marketing."

Any arbitrary content will not suffice. In order to retain their continuous engagement and, of equal significance, elicit a desirable response towards the affiliate links embedded within your content, it is crucial to ensure the provision of high-quality content.

8. Utilize data analytics to evaluate and quantify your achievements

Regard analytics as a tool that furnishes insights into your sales activities, encompassing details on the products or services sold, the manner in which they were sold, and the targeted audience to whom they were sold. Fortunately, most affiliate marketing sites provide comprehensive analytics which can be immensely useful. They will perform a comprehensive analysis of all the data gathered from your website and provide you with insights regarding its effectiveness and areas for improvement.

If your objective is to gain insights into the demographics of your website visitors, Google Analytics emerges as the most reliable choice. Upon gaining insight into the demographic, it becomes feasible to devise targeted content.

Additionally, it is important to diligently observe posts that attract the greatest number of visitors. One might consider incorporating affiliate marketing links into posts that are experiencing higher levels of traffic.

If you have a genuine commitment to pursuing affiliate marketing, it is imperative that you ascertain the strategies and tactics that yield favorable results and allocate your focus accordingly. Remove what doesn't work. You can find out what types of ads are working for you and what aren't through the analytics that the company provides. Naturally, it is advisable to utilize the functioning ones and eliminate the non-functioning ones.

9. Make the necessary arrangements for filing taxes

In the event that commissions are being generated through the practice of affiliate marketing, whether it be at a gradual but consistent pace, taxation obligations will need to be fulfilled.

Ultimately, it constitutes revenue. The corporations with which you have established alliances will forward a 1099 form to you in the early stages of the year. Nevertheless, refrain from awaiting their action. Please ensure that you duly report your income to the Internal Revenue Service (IRS) within the specified time frame.

If your method of operating as an affiliate marketer is through the structure of either a sole proprietorship or limited liability company (LLC), it is necessary for you to disclose the generated 1099 income on Schedule C – Profit or Loss from Business.

Alternatively, in the event that your business is operating under the structure of a C or S corporation, it is necessary to declare the earnings on Schedule K1.

10. Expand Your Business

Your enterprise will either experience growth or downsizing in the future. This is the rationale behind the necessity of growth. If the diminishing of returns impacts your business, you will need to continue reducing.

Do not limit yourself to exclusively marketing a single product. Persist in the search for novel merchandise that can be marketed. Continue navigating through the various affiliate websites. Additionally, ensure that you remain vigilant for emerging enterprises that have recently initiated affiliate marketing initiatives. In the event that they possess an opportunity that you deem suitable, consider initiating a collaboration with them.

Furthermore, it is advisable to consistently and regularly engage in online promotional activities for your business. You have the option to utilize electronic correspondence, social media platforms, and diverse marketing strategies to promote your business, thereby fostering customer loyalty through the consistent provision of advantageous offers on the company's promoted services and products.

11. Entrust Laborious Assignments to Others

After your affiliate marketing efforts begin to generate a positive financial outcome, it will be imperative to prioritize expansion. This implies that you will also be required to assign the routine tasks to another individual. Certainly, this entails the recruitment of labor which consequently leads to additional costs; nevertheless, the ultimate outcome justifies the investment. The delegation will provide you with sufficient time to devise alternative approaches for promoting your business and maximizing its growth potential.

12. Employ Automation to Simplify Tasks

Digital marketing tools can effectively alleviate your workload, thus enabling you to divert your focus towards other facets of your business. The majority of these tools require payment, yet the return on investment justifies the expenditure.

The primary objective is to allow you to direct your focus towards business expansion, as your employees and tools efficiently manage the operational tasks.

Prior to delving into the realm of affiliate networks, it is prudent to examine various means of assessing the product or service one opts for.

Advantages Of Affiliate Marketing

Affiliate marketing is gaining traction as a widely accepted approach in online marketing due to its cost-effectiveness and potential for substantial returns. Affiliate marketing can be utilized as a means to promote and market a wide range of products, services, or organizations.

The advantages of affiliate marketing are numerous and diverse, with a particularly prominent aspect being its cost-effective nature as a means to promote products. Frequently, affiliates are afforded the chance to promote products in which they possess a certain affiliation - either through personal usage or association with others who utilize them. As a result of this, they become significantly more engaged in the sales of these products, leading to improved outcomes for all parties concerned.

There exist several advantages derived from engaging in Affiliate Marketing, which include the following:

affiliate marketing are:

• It is more cost-effective compared to the majority of alternative advertising methods.

• It allows small businesses to attain a level playing field for promoting their products and services.

• Remuneration based on commissions - Affiliate marketers receive their compensation through a structure that is dependent on performance or a predetermined payment per completed sale.

• Zero initial expenses - Given the absence of any required upfront investments for individuals seeking to promote a product or service via affiliate marketing, there are no associated costs at the outset.

- Absence of extensive inventory - This facilitates the involvement of companies of varying scales, ranging from small-scale startups to large corporations, in affiliate marketing without the burden of significant expenses.

- It provides an opportunity for entrepreneurs with limited financial resources to market their products or services.

- There are no initial expenses or stock required.

- This opportunity allows individuals to engage in it either on a part-time basis in addition to their regular commitments or to commit to it on a full-time basis, thereby creating an additional source of income.

- The possibility of earning generous commission rates

- There is no requirement for physical workspace, personnel, or stock • Exclusion of the necessity for an office environment, staff members, or goods in storage • The absence of a necessity for office premises, human resources, or merchandise • Elimination of the need for a physical office, employees, or inventory

In addition, it is customary for affiliate marketers to possess their individual website where prospective visitors can conveniently subscribe to content updates through RSS feeds or email notifications. Moreover, they can partake in specialized forums wherein discussions related to their offerings are actively conducted. Affiliate marketing proves to be a lucrative online avenue, highly favored by digital entrepreneurs.

Chapter 5: Terminology of Affiliate Marketing Glossary

- Affiliates are individuals, including publishers such as yourself and myself, who utilize affiliate program links to effectively promote products and generate sales.

➤ Affiliate marketplace: Numerous online platforms, such as ShareASale, CJ (Commission Junction), Clickbank, JVzoo, function as expansive centralized repositories for diverse affiliate programs within various niche markets.

⊙ Affiliate software: Software utilized by businesses to establish an affiliate program for their merchandise. Ex: iDevaffiliate.

⊙ Referral link: A customized tracking URL provided by your affiliate program to monitor the effectiveness of your online affiliate marketing campaign.

⊙ Affiliate Identification: Correspondingly to the notion of an affiliate link, numerous affiliate programs provide a distinctive identification code, commonly known as an affiliate ID. This alphanumeric code can be appended to any webpage within the product's website, signifying your affiliation as an affiliate marketer.

- Payment method: Each affiliate program provides its own unique payment options, which may vary across different platforms. For example: Methods such as cheque, wire transfer, PayPal, and numerous others can be utilized.

- Affiliation Coordinator: Numerous enterprises engage specialized affiliation coordinators to assist publishers in enhancing their earnings, while providing them with optimization strategies.

- Standard commission rate: The foundational rate applied to a specified program term.

- Commission rate: The rate at which you will receive a portion of the sales amount for each completed sale facilitated through your affiliate link program.

- Two-tier affiliate marketing: This method presents a highly effective means of generating income through involvement in an affiliate program. Within this context, you advocate for the enrollment of individuals into affiliate programs, with the proposition that you shall receive a commission when sales are generated by the sub-affiliate. It bears some similarities to the MLM (Multi-level) marketing model. This term is commonly referred to as Sub-affiliate Commission.

⊛ Website homepage(s): A distinctive webpage dedicated to promoting and showcasing a product in order to enhance sales. The majority of the programs that you will be promoting are equipped with multiple landing pages.

⊛ Tailored Affiliate Compensation/ account: In contrast to a standard affiliate account, numerous companies extend custom affiliate compensation plans to individuals who generate the highest volume of affiliate sales for their organization.

⊛ Link obfuscation: The majority of affiliate tracking links possess unattractive appearances, often being excessively long and containing special characters. Through the implementation of link obfuscation techniques, it becomes possible to transform these unsightly links into easily understandable and user-friendly formats.

⦿ Cost-per-action, also known as cost per action (CPA), refers to a quantitative measure employed in online advertising, whereby a predetermined rate is established for each user-initiated action. Instances of cost-per-action (CPA) transactions encompass cost per click, cost per lead, and cost per sale.

⦿ Pay-per-click, pay per click (PPC): A remuneration model whereby an advertiser compensates its publishers a fixed fee each time a user clicks on a hyperlink present on the publisher's website and gets directed to the advertiser's website. See also pay-per-click.

- Cost-per-lead, cost per lead (CPL): A remuneration arrangement wherein advertisers provide a fixed payment to publishers for each eligible customer lead obtained through a hyperlink on the publisher's website or websites.

- Cost-per-thousand impressions (CPM): A remuneration model commonly applied in the advertising industry, wherein the advertiser compensates a fixed fee for each batch of 1000 impressions delivered. As an illustration, consider the case where a website levies a fee of $1,000 per advertisement and states that it has received 100,000 visits, resulting in a CPM of $10. Additionally known as "cost-per-thousand."

- Acquisition: A circumstance that arises when a website visitor clicks on a hyperlink and completes a purchase, generates a lead, or generates sales for an advertiser. Publishers receive commissions upon the occurrence of conversions.

- Personalized vouchers: Numerous corporate initiatives provide affiliates with the opportunity to generate customized vouchers, which serve the dual purpose of sales monitoring. Additionally, the utilization of personalized discount vouchers serves to facilitate the growth of affiliate sales. If you are generating a significant volume of sales for a specific merchant, it is appropriate to inquire about the possibility of obtaining an exclusive coupon for your personal use.

- Commission rate: The remuneration offered by advertisers to publishers, either as a fixed amount or a percentage of the total transaction value, typically denominated in currency.

- Commission: The remuneration granted to a publisher by an advertiser as an incentivization for generating leads or sales via its website or blog.

A company can derive advantages from participating in an affiliate program, as it presents one of the most effective means of obtaining complimentary promotion and achieving some measure of savings on advertising expenses.

For instance, when encountering promotional vouchers or reduced-price hyperlinks, it is common for these links to be affiliated ones that offer monetary benefits upon completing a purchase.

Chapter 6: In-Depth Examination of Essential Characteristics for Ensuring the Success of an Affiliate Program

Each affiliate program and platform has its own unique characteristics and distinctions.

Distinct in the aspects of affiliate requirements, policies, and remuneration structures for affiliates such as ourselves.

Particularly when embarking on a new affiliation program, it is crucial to seek out specific attributes that should be inherent in their partnership.

Chapter 7: Methodology for Payment Options

This option holds significant importance and merits early discussion, as each platform possesses its own distinct payment system, thereby exhibiting variations between them.

Certain individuals choose to remunerate you through various methods such as Paypal, cash, or Cheque, the nature of which hinges on your selection of a payment option within the affiliate program.

Chapter 8: Utilizing Affiliate Links for Singular Products

When incorporating product affiliate links into your website or blog, or when enrolling in an affiliate program for your website or blog, it is crucial that each affiliate program or product provides a unique link for their respective products.

In order for potential customers or users to be redirected to your sales homepage, they will be directed to the specific page highlighting your product for sale.

Given the paramount importance of your sales page.

Chapter Nine: Gaining Access to Affiliate Statistics and Promotional Banners.

Please compile comprehensive statistics regarding all significant entities within an affiliate program, including affiliates, campaigns, and even banners, providing a thorough analysis for each category of information.

Endeavor to become part of their organization, which boasts a comprehensive affiliate platform granting you the ability to monitor every individual sale, generate reports, and assess the effectiveness of your promotional strategies through a user-friendly administrative panel designed specifically for affiliates.

Chapter 10: Comparing Affiliate Marketing and Adsense for Alternative Monetization

Primarily, the choice between utilizing Google AdSense or affiliate marketing for website or blog monetization on a multi-niche platform relies on individual preference and personal opinion.

If your niche blog is aligned with a relevant product, implementing affiliate marketing can prove to be highly advantageous for you.

When commencing our venture into Affiliate marketing, the initial inquiry often arises regarding whether we should prioritize Affiliate programs or Google AdSense, commonly denoted as Cost Per Click (CPC).

In the upcoming chapter, I will present a reflection of my recent experiences pertaining to both strategies, namely Google AdSense and Affiliate, offering you the opportunity to discern the approach that best aligns with your objectives.

You have the option to select among various models, such as utilizing Affiliate marketing banners, Google AdSense, or Direct advertisements, in order to monetize your website or blog.

I have noticed that individuals often hold a prevailing misconception regarding Search Engines, particularly Google, assuming that they are adversarial towards affiliate marketing links and programming. However, I would like to clarify that this notion is merely a fallacy or misunderstanding. The reality is that no search engine opposes these practices.

According to the majority of search engines, it is advisable to retain the affiliate link, provided that it is hosted on a reputable website or blog of high quality.

Engaging in the creation of manipulative and subpar content, coupled with excessive utilization of affiliate links, has the potential to detrimentally impact both the search engine ranking and the esteemed reputation of your website.

ASSESSING APPROPRIATE AFFILIATES (ALONG WITH ONES TO BE CAUTIOUS OF)

After the completion of the product creation phase, it is appropriate to establish an independent affiliate program in order to optimize the extent of your market penetration. Having your own affiliate program is akin to having a dedicated workforce of sales representatives consistently present on your website, actively contributing to the growth and development of your business. Nevertheless, securing suitable affiliates demands careful contemplation and deliberation.

Quality trumps quantity.

If your associates lack strong sales skills, the quantity of 1000 affiliates will not contribute to your success. The utilization of unethical tactics by individuals involved in the promotion of your product can equally engender adverse consequences for your brand. By directing your attention towards recruiting high-quality affiliates instead of a large quantity of affiliates, you can effectively mitigate the majority of potential issues related to affiliate programs.

Their internet site

Review the websites of all prospective candidates. Do they consistently update and curate a blog? Does the content align with the needs and preferences of your intended demographic? Can I be assured of the safety and security of the website? Are they in compliance with all relevant laws pertaining to spam, privacy, and other matters in both their country and yours? According to the information provided on the website, does it seem that they possess integrity and assurance?

Their Web Address

Conducting a "Who Is" search is an effective method to acquire further information regarding the individual responsible for the website. The data shall be concealed within select websites. Should this situation arise, it is advisable to conduct further investigation to ascertain the credibility of the individuals behind the website, ensuring that they are individuals of integrity with whom you would find it suitable to engage in face-to-face business transactions.

The data and materials furnished by them" "The information and content disseminated by them" "The facts and resources made available by them" "The knowledge and substance offered by them

Upon perusing the website and acquainting oneself with its content and information, does one perceive a persuasive appeal towards the intended audience, increasing the likelihood of their inclination to engage in a purchase from said entity? What are the specific categories of keywords that they utilize? Do the subjects addressed and the information presented exhibit a direct and truthful nature? Considering your mother's need for information, would you assess the website as a secure and reliable source to direct her towards?

Financial Validation

Upon acquiring an affiliate, it is imperative to ensure their completion of all requisite legal documentation. In the event that you opt not to issue 1099s due to utilizing a third-party payment service such as PayPal, it remains crucial to obtain that pertinent information. Doing so not only affirms the legitimacy of recipients, but also aids in upholding customer safety by validating their credentials. Furthermore, can they demonstrate a history of achievement in the field of affiliate marketing?

When embarking on your journey as a product seller, it may be impractical to exercise complete selectivity in choosing affiliates. Nevertheless, it is imperative to ensure, at the very minimum, that individuals seeking to become affiliates are able to authenticate their identities, possess no criminal background, and conduct business with customers in a manner that upholds integrity and transparency. It is important to note that selecting individuals with limited experience in affiliate marketing will necessitate the provision of training and motivation to ensure their proficiency in generating sales.

Comprehending The Payment Mechanism Utilized By Clickbank

Affiliate marketers seeking a streamlined method of working from their residences can avail themselves of the affiliate programs provided by Clickbank. One key benefit is that the process of registering as an affiliate is both effortless and complimentary.

For individuals who are new to the field of affiliate marketing, the concept of generating income through the promotion of others' products may initially appear perplexing. To engage with Clickbank, it is necessary to commence by registering and subsequently identifying a selection of products to endorse. Subsequently, it is essential to generate a Hoplink and commence the promotion of the products.

When a customer observes the Hoplink and chooses to interact with it, they are redirected to the website of the publisher. In the eventuality that the aforementioned customer engages in a purchase, thereby facilitating the acquisition of said product, you shall be entitled to receive your designated commission.

The commission you will receive is contingent upon the selling price of the product you have successfully marketed, and it will be promptly credited to your account approximately two to three minutes following the completion of the sale.

It should be worth noting that each and every Clickbank product has a commission rate. The commission rate is determined by the publisher or vendor of the product and can range from 1% to 75% of the product's selling price. The highest commission that you could potentially earn per product is $150.

After a customer purchases a product that you have promoted, Clickbank assumes responsibility for managing the payment transactions. It subsequently applies any fees to the sale and calculates your commission based on the net value of the sale." or "Upon the completion of a customer's purchase of a product promoted by you, Clickbank assumes the role of facilitator for the payment transactions. Following this, it deducts any applicable fees from the sale and proceeds to calculate your commission based on the net value of the transaction.

To be eligible for the disbursement of your initial commission earnings, it is imperative that you satisfy two prescribed prerequisites. Initially, you must meet the specified payment threshold that you have personally established within your account settings. Furthermore, it is imperative that you fulfill the stipulated criteria outlined in the Customer Distribution Requirement. In the event that you fulfill both criteria, you may commence the receipt of your earned commissions.

Upon receipt of two checks through regular mail from Clickbank, you will be qualified to receive direct deposit of your earnings directly into your account.

One crucial factor to bear in mind is that in the event of a product being returned by a customer or a request for a refund, it will not be possible to receive your commission. Clickbank will initiate the reimbursement of funds to the customer, ensuring that both your share of earnings and the vendor's portion are duly restored. Clickbank employs a return allowance policy to address instances pertaining to reimbursements and product returns.

To fully exploit Clickbank's dependable payment system, it is imperative to ensure effective promotion of your selected products. It all begins with the selection of products to endorse.

Upon the establishment of your Clickbank account, it is essential to peruse the marketplace and identify products that you confidently believe have the potential for effective promotion. It is necessary to verify the gravitational properties of the product. Ideally, it is recommended to select a product with a gravity of 50 or more in order to maximize its potential for successful sales. Nevertheless, this should not impede your ability to select a product with lesser significance if you genuinely believe in your capacity to effectively market and sell the said product.

Upon selecting a product, it is imperative to consider strategies for effectively promoting said product. There exists a multitude of approaches through which this can be accomplished. If you possess proficient writing skills, you may consider engaging in article marketing. This indicates that you will be composing articles pertaining to the specific category in which your product is classified and subsequently submitting them to article directories.

In the section where the director requests the author's biography, it is permissible to incorporate details regarding your product alongside a hyperlink that showcases your affiliate identification. Once a reader of the article clicks on the link, they will be directed to either the landing page of the product vendor or the landing page of your own site.

To fully exploit the benefits of article writing, it is imperative to submit articles to multiple article directories to extensively diversify your promotional endeavors.

The final step will indisputably constitute the primary focus of this article. After completing the article, your goal should be to maximize its exposure through various channels. In this particular sequence, kindly proceed to deliver to these designated websites. There exists a plethora of online platforms solely dedicated to the acceptance of articles, on the condition that said articles possess qualities of high caliber and are devoid of any plagiarized content previously published by others.

You can also promote your product via social networking. You have the ability to develop a dedicated page for your product and promote it among your acquaintances, which will consequently amplify the visibility of your promotional endeavors to their networks and beyond.

There exists a plethora of online methods by which one may engage in product promotion and one is at liberty to explore and harness the potential benefits of these techniques. Please bear in mind that as a product receives greater visibility, its chances of being purchased increase. Consequently, once a sale is made, you will be entitled to earn a commission based on the sales made. Your earnings will increase in proportion to the number of sales you make.

Clickbank, the preeminent online marketplace, is a highly efficient platform that enables individuals to generate income through the promotion of third-party products. Even though the task of advertising a product may require significant exertion, it implies that you are marketing an already established product and therefore do not have to concern yourself with its creation.

Furthermore, it is cost-effective to become a Clickbank affiliate as no fees are required to enroll in the program. Clickbank presents a remarkable opportunity for substantial earnings through the convenience of remote work, where you can engage in the sales of pre-existing products within the confines of your own home. This is facilitated by a range of tools available to you, graciously provided by the publishers and vendors in the majority of circumstances.

Clickbank additionally ensures the regular and prompt disbursement of commission income that rightfully belongs to you, allowing you to fully reap the rewards of your hard work.

Now, this marks the conclusion of the initial phase of this guide. Let us proceed to the subsequent stage and commence the actual implementation, wherein we will thoroughly explore the marketplace and acquire the skills to identify a markedly lucrative product.

Lets get started!

Strategies For Prudently Evaluating Affiliate Products And Making Informed Decisions

Affiliate marketing is a highly accessible and efficient method of generating online income; however, it is not devoid of any inherent risks. Namely, should you opt for the wrong product or employ a misguided advertising approach, the anticipated expeditious success may elude you. This is a point worth considering.

Should this be the situation, a substantial portion of your forthcoming achievements will rely on your ability to discern and choose the suitable product. Enclosed herewith is the information that is essential for your perusal.

Items That Should Not Be Offered for Sale

When consumers undertake the task of selecting a product to retail, a significant majority tend to commence by accessing their favored affiliate network (such as ClickBank, JVZoo, WSOPro), subsequently seeking out products that exhibit the highest sales figures and offer the most substantial commission rates.

This is an intelligent strategy as the data suggests that a substantial income is being earned by others, indicating that it is feasible for you to attain a similar degree of financial prosperity. Indeed, it is feasible to replicate their business model by utilizing a technique commonly known as "cut and paste."

Nevertheless, if that is the sole activity you are partaking in, it constitutes engaging in improper conduct. A vast majority, approximately ninety-nine percent, of the products that occupy the uppermost positions in the listing pertain to specific subjects, namely dating, fitness, or online wealth generation.

By commencing the promotion of one of these books, you will henceforth encounter competition not only from other sellers offering the very same book, but also from those selling comparable books. The overwhelming majority of individuals who have been involved in online activities for a period exceeding 24 hours are fatigued with the incessant promotion of "earn money from the comfort of your own residence" schemes.

Furthermore, each of these subfields exhibits a high level of competitiveness within the online sphere. If you do not possess a highly prosperous website or mailing list, it will be exceedingly challenging for you to attain the coveted position on Google's search results page for the key phrases "Make Money Online eBook" or "Build Muscle." By adhering to this approach, you are inadvertently depriving yourself of an opportunity to achieve success.

Alternative Strategies

Alternatively, you should consider choosing a product that aligns with a more niche market. Suppose you come across an electronic book that caters to a specific profession or sector, such as a guide on generating income through floral arrangement. The size of the audience is comparatively smaller, giving the impression of reduced interest; however, this ultimately renders your offering entirely unique.

Furthermore, it is possible to conveniently establish contact with those individuals responsible for arranging flowers by sharing your thoughts and inquiries on multiple floral blogs. It is expected that the process of positioning your sales page at the forefront of Google's search results for the specific keyword "flower arranging eBook" would be significantly easier. Furthermore, it possesses a distinctive and compelling unique selling proposition (USP) that simplifies the selling process.

It would be prudent to conduct an analysis of the existing distribution channels at your disposal. With whom are you acquainted, from whom you could derive maximum benefit? In which location can one find the highest concentration of individuals? What are the interests of those individuals?

Prior to finalizing a product choice, it is advisable to carefully consider the distribution channels that will be utilized and the specific target markets where your discerning customers are most likely to be found. This is the methodology that will pave the path to accomplishment, one which you can employ repeatedly.

If you currently possess a thriving website that garners a significant amount of traffic

CHAPTER 3

Given the presence of a diverse consumer demographic, it is essential to choose a product that will effectively captivate the attention of your established customer base.

Multiple Products

Please bear in mind that there is also the option to sell a substantial quantity of items. In the context of offering digital products, an advantageous aspect of this business model is the ability to swiftly incorporate or remove elements from your website, thereby obviating the necessity of devoting extensive time to content creation and preparation.

There are pros and cons to offering a diverse range of products. If your website is of considerable size and you employ persuasive strategies, it behooves you to offer a diverse range of products for sale (refer to the subsequent chapter). As a consequence of this, you possess the capability to offer a diverse range of price points that can accommodate the needs and preferences of a wide spectrum of consumers.

With that being said, by focusing your attention on one product at a time, you can generate greater enthusiasm and excitement surrounding that specific product, while also designing a more efficient website that directs clients to a single page - namely, the page where they can complete their purchase.

Opting to Acquire Physical Commodities

The process of choosing physical objects differs slightly. Once more, it is advisable to adopt a strategy wherein you carefully select items that pertain to both the content presented on your website and the demographic of individuals who typically engage with said content.

Simultaneously, these must be items of excellent craftsmanship and that fulfill a legitimate need within the market.

Fortunately, there is no requirement to make an initial investment of a substantial sum and to undertake a gamble by purchasing a large quantity of items all at once. Rest assured that you will not encounter the situation of possessing a fully stocked warehouse solely dedicated to fidget spinners.

This suggests that you have the liberty to embrace prevailing trends and, in a broader sense, experiment with various approaches to test their effectiveness.

Nevertheless, if your objective is to cater to a diverse clientele, it is imperative that you offer a diverse range of products and services, spanning across different price points. This will enable you to attract a broad spectrum of buyers.

Additionally, it is important to note that you will receive a commission for each product bought after the visitor has accessed Amazon. This signifies that the foremost objective should be to encourage the customer to click on the link and access the page, sometimes even prioritizing this over the actual sale of the specific item under consideration.

Establish your own website and enlist yourself with a web hosting provider. Establish a fresh webpage and proceed to include the acquired sales page copy alongside your affiliate link. Having acquired all the necessary resources, you are now equipped to commence the process of marketing your merchandise and generating financial gains through successful transactions. Subsequently, the subsequent chapter will delve into the subsequent task that necessitates prompt action.

What are the advantages of pursuing a career in affiliate marketing?

What factors contribute to one's decision to pursue a career as an affiliate marketer?

1. Passive income.

While conventional employment necessitates physical presence for monetary gain, affiliate marketing offers the opportunity to generate income even during periods of rest. By allocating a specific time frame to a marketing initiative, you will experience a consistent yield on that expenditure as customers make purchases in the subsequent days and weeks.

Compensation for your task is received considerably after its completion. Despite not being physically present at a computer, your marketing abilities will continuously generate a steady flow of financial resources for you.

2. No customer support.

Personal vendors and enterprises engaged in the trade of goods or services have a responsibility to engage with their clientele to ensure their utmost satisfaction in their transactions.

Thanks to the implementation of the affiliate marketing framework, concerns regarding customer service and satisfaction will never be a cause for worry. The primary objective of the affiliate marketer is to establish a connection between the vendor and the customer. The seller assumes responsibility for addressing any consumer complaints once you have received your commission resulting from the sale.

3. Work from home.

If you happen to harbor disdain for the prospect of going to work, affiliate marketing presents itself as a fitting alternative for your consideration. From the convenience of your own residence, you will have the opportunity to initiate campaigns and generate income from the products crafted by sellers. This position can be executed from the comfort of your home attire.

4. Cost-effective.

The majority of corporations necessitate initial expenditures and ongoing cash inflows to facilitate the financing of their merchandise offerings. In contrast, affiliate marketing presents a cost-effective approach, enabling swift launch and requiring minimal exertion. There are no associated expenses to concern oneself with in relation to affiliate programs, and there is no requirement to engage in product manufacturing. Commencing operations in this industry can be accomplished with relative ease.

5. Convenient and flexible.

Given that you will essentially be assuming the role of a self-employed professional, you will enjoy absolute autonomy in setting your objectives, adjusting your trajectory when necessary, choosing products that align with your interests, and even establishing your own work schedule. Due to this adaptable nature, you have the option to broaden the range of your investment portfolio or adhere to straightforward and uncomplicated campaigns. You will no longer be subjected to stringent rules and regulations, nor will you have to deal with underperforming teams.

6. Performance-Based rewards.

Alternate phrase: "In alternative occupations, individuals have the opportunity to work up to 70 hours per week while still earning an equivalent income." Success in affiliate marketing hinges entirely on your performance. The outcome will be commensurate with the effort you invest in it. Enhancing your review skills and crafting compelling marketing content will lead to immediate increments in income.

Your exceptional dedication will be duly remunerated.

7. Do not underestimate the influence that SEO possesses.

By employing proper SEO techniques, one can acquire a significant volume of organic traffic through search engine referrals. The era in which Search Engine Optimization (SEO) primarily revolved around deceiving Google has long since passed. The current focus revolves around enhancing the user-friendliness of your website. Individuals are inherently inclined towards accessing the internet as a source of information.

In order to position yourself as the primary source of information, it is imperative to acquire a solid understanding of on-page SEO techniques, keyword analysis, and the cultivation of links. Who wouldn't aspire to attain the topmost position on Google search results for highly sought-after phrases such as "best product" or "product review"?

www.ingramcontent.com/pod-product-compliance
Lightning Source LLC
Chambersburg PA
CBHW050240120526
44590CB00016B/2169